Willa Cather

Writer of Pioneer Stories

Tammy Orr Staats

Boston, Massachusetts
Chandler, Arizona
Glenview, Illinois
Upper Saddle River, New Jersey

Illustrations
8, 9, 10, 12, 15 Mike Lacey; 7 Joe LeMonnier.

Photographs
Every effort has been made to secure permission and provide appropriate credit for photographic material.
The publisher deeply regrets any omission and pledges to correct errors called to its attention in subsequent editions.

Unless otherwise acknowledged, all photographs are the property of Pearson Education, Inc.

Photo locators denoted as follows: Top (T), Center (C), Bottom (B), Left (L), Right (R), Background (Bkgd)

Opener: (Bkgrd) Jupiterimages/Thinkstock, (Inset) Prints & Photographs Division, LC-USZ62-82912/Library of Congress;
1 Prints & Photographs Division, LC-USZ62-82912/Library of Congress; 2 Prints & Photographs Division, LC-USZ62-82912/
Library of Congress; 3 An American Time Capsule, Rare Book and Special Collections Division, rbpe13401300/Library of
Congress; 4 Jupiterimages/Thinkstock; 5 Prints & Photographs Division, LC-DIG-ppmsca-08378/Library of Congress; 6 FSA/
OWI Collection, Prints & Photographs Division, LC-USF34-008666-D/Library of Congress; 11 Prints & Photographs Division,
LC-DIG-ppmsca-08375 /Library of Congress; 13 FSA/OWI Collection, Prints & Photographs Division, LC-USF33-001468-M3/
Library of Congress.

ISBN-13: 978-0-328-67644-6
ISBN-10:   0-328-67644-6

9 10 11 V0SI 17 16 15

Willa Cather

Writer of Pioneer Stories

Tammy Orr Staats

Boston, Massachusetts
Chandler, Arizona
Glenview, Illinois
Upper Saddle River, New Jersey

Illustrations
8, 9, 10, 12, 15 Mike Lacey; 7 Joe LeMonnier.

Photographs
Every effort has been made to secure permission and provide appropriate credit for photographic material.
The publisher deeply regrets any omission and pledges to correct errors called to its attention in subsequent editions.

Unless otherwise acknowledged, all photographs are the property of Pearson Education, Inc.

Photo locators denoted as follows: Top (T), Center (C), Bottom (B), Left (L), Right (R), Background (Bkgd)

Opener: (Bkgd) Jupiterimages/Thinkstock, (Inset) Prints & Photographs Division, LC-USZ62-82912/Library of Congress;
1 Prints & Photographs Division, LC-USZ62-82912/Library of Congress; 2 Prints & Photographs Division, LC-USZ62-82912/
Library of Congress; 3 An American Time Capsule, Rare Book and Special Collections Division, rbpe13401300/Library of
Congress; 4 Jupiterimages/Thinkstock; 5 Prints & Photographs Division, LC-DIG-ppmsca-08378/Library of Congress; 6 FSA/
OWI Collection, Prints & Photographs Division, LC-USF34-008666-D/Library of Congress; 11 Prints & Photographs Division,
LC-DIG-ppmsca-08375 /Library of Congress; 13 FSA/OWI Collection, Prints & Photographs Division, LC-USF33-001468-M3/
Library of Congress.

ISBN-13: 978-0-328-67644-6
ISBN-10: 0-328-67644-6

9 10 11 V0SI 17 16 15

A Famous Writer

In 1883, Willa Cather's family left the hills and trees of Virginia and headed west. In Nebraska they found a wide, flat **prairie**. There were tall grasses as far as the eye could see. Families from many places settled there. All had come hoping for a better life.

Willa Cather later became famous. She wrote about this land and the people who came to live there.

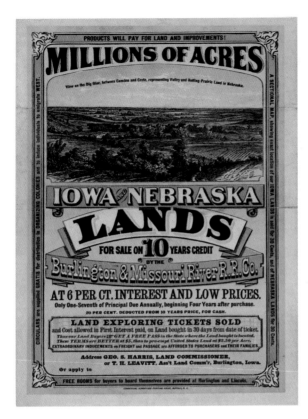

One of many advertisements for land

Early Years

The oldest of seven children, Willa Cather was born in Virginia in 1873. Cather's uncle had recently moved west. More and more people were moving there as well. People said that the prairie of the Midwest offered good land that was easy to farm. The prairie offered them the promise of a new life.

The Big Move

In the spring of 1883, Willa Cather, age 9, and her family made their way across the country by train. Cather was startled by what she saw. Instead of rolling hills and leafy trees, she saw bare fields of tall grass. She felt as if she had been "thrown into a country as bare as a piece of sheet iron."

The wide, flat prairie

A sod house made of grass and dirt

A New Life

The Cathers lived in a wood-framed house. They were lucky. Some families lived in houses made of blocks of **sod**. Life was hard for these **pioneers**. Often, people battled harsh weather. Some lost their farms because of lack of farming experience. In spite of all this, young Cather found herself falling in love with the Nebraska prairie.

A typical one-room schoolhouse

As a girl, Willa Cather attended a one-room schoolhouse. However, her most valuable education came from spending time with the **immigrants** she met. Cather came to appreciate them and respect their different ways of life.

A Second Move

After almost a year, Cather's father had had enough of farming. He moved his family to the town of Red Cloud and became a businessman.

Cather loved town life. She enjoyed the music and shows she found there. She met an Englishman who taught her to read Greek and Latin. A Jewish family from Europe let her borrow books.

The Cather Family Homes

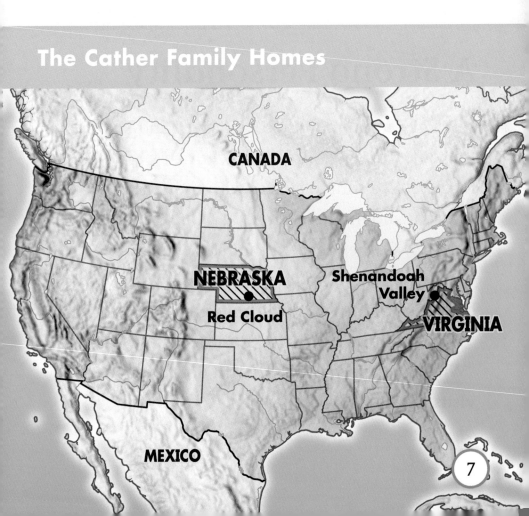

CANADA

NEBRASKA

Shenandoah Valley

Red Cloud

VIRGINIA

MEXICO

The Cather family home in Red Cloud, Nebraska, still stands today.

A Strong Personality

At 11, Cather got a job delivering mail. Along the way, Cather stopped and chatted with the farmers. She shared stories with the immigrant women who interested her.

At 15, Cather decided that she wanted to be a doctor. There were few female doctors in those days, but Cather was determined. She called herself "Wm. Cather, M.D." *Wm.* is short for the name "William." She went with local doctors on their visits to sick people.

Becoming a Writer

When she graduated from school, Cather was given an honor. She proudly gave the graduation speech. Then she headed off to the University of Nebraska. She still hoped to study medicine.

Something happened to change her plans. Without telling her, a professor sent an **essay** she wrote to a newspaper. Then she got the news. Her essay was going to be published! Now Cather declared that she wanted to become a writer.

The University of Nebraska

9

After college, Cather was a writer and teacher.
Then, in 1911, Cather decided to focus just on
writing. Her first **novel**, published in 1912, was not
very successful. Then she decided she would write
about what she knew best—the people and places
of the prairie.

O Pioneers!

Cather's second novel was a great success. *O Pioneers!* tells the story of Alexandra Bergman. She is the daughter of an immigrant from Norway. Before her father dies, he asks her to take over the family farm.

For many readers, Cather's stories felt real because she'd seen it all firsthand. Her characters have courage and spirit, just like the pioneers Cather knew as a child.

A pioneer family

My Ántonia

In 1918, Cather released her fourth novel, *My Ántonia*. Many people consider it her best book. Cather wrote about how pioneers struggled to adapt to their new lives.

The book tells the story of an immigrant family that comes from Europe. The father is never able to adjust to pioneer life. Once he had been a musician. Now he is a farmer living in a sod house. He doesn't know the first thing about farming. Every day, he insists on getting dressed up in clothes that he wore in the "old country." The book describes how hard it was for immigrants to adapt to life in a new country.

My Ántonia was published in 1918.

MY ÁNTONIA
BY
WILLA S. CATHER

Cather based her characters on the people she met in the Midwest.

Cather's Writing

Cather's characters, like Cather herself, felt a strong link to the land on which they lived. Cather's writing was unusual for the time. The language was plain and simple, just like the lives of her characters. Telling the stories of these pioneers was Cather's great gift to her readers.

A Great Honor

With the publication of each new book, Cather became more well respected and well known. In 1922, Cather won the Pulitzer Prize. This is one of the biggest honors an American writer can receive.

Timeline of Willa Cather's Life

1873
Cather is born in Virginia.

1884
Cather's family moves to the town of Red Cloud.

1913
Cather publishes *O Pioneers!*

1870   1880   1890   1900

1883
Cather's family moves to a farm in Nebraska.

1891
Cather begins to attend University of Nebraska.

Willa Cather died on April 24, 1947, in New York City. The girl who so wanted to become a doctor had become a famous writer instead. No matter where she traveled, Cather never forgot the wide, grassy prairie that was her home when she was a child.

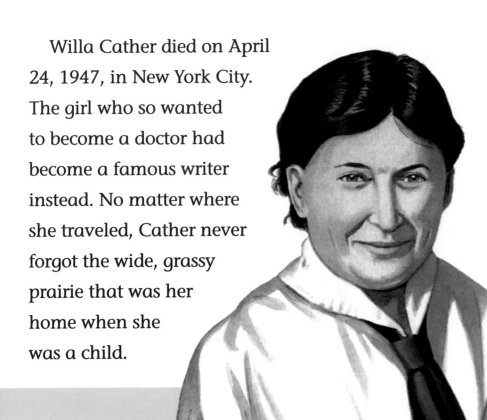

1922
Cather wins the
Pulitzer Prize.

1920   **1930**   **1940**   **1950**

1918
Cather publishes
My Antonia.

1947
Cather dies in
New York City.

Glossary

essay a short piece of nonfiction writing on a specific topic

immigrant a person who moves to a new country

novel a long fictional story by a writer

pioneer someone who is among the first people to settle in a new area

prairie a large, mostly flat, area of grassland without trees

sod soil covered with thick grass